A DECADE OF TRANSITION

*A Collection of the Poems
of David Williams, 2004–2014*

Published in South Africa

A Morgan & Masterson Publication

Morgan & Masterson LLC, One Sheffield Place, Winston-Salem, NC 27104 USA
info@morgan-masterson.com
www.morgan-masterson.com

A Decade of Transition

ISBN 978-0-620-70686-5
Copyright © David Franklyn Williams
David Williams, Sala Kahli Lodge, La Ferme Chantelle, Franschhoek, South
Africa

First edition: 2016

Copy edited and proofread by Liz Sparg
Cover design and cover artwork by Design for development
Author image by Peggy O'Donnell
Other images by David Williams

INTRODUCTION

After many years of working as a scientist, writing papers and books, editing journals and thinking and living as a scientist, I am used to articulating my thoughts and conclusions, although not my feelings, in a rigorous and dignified way; indeed in what some might describe as a turgid, impersonal way. In most scientific arenas there is no room for sentiment, unproven facts and personal bias.

That had to change, as I wanted to express myself in a different way, without affecting my professional style or, indeed, my reputation. How could I do this? I am Welsh, but my Celtic heritage had, until quite recently, been only a nascent influence on my life. So there was the answer, perhaps; the poetry of the bards, the lyrical sentences of the Celtic style, had no pretentions to scientific formality – it was just uninhibited expression of thought.

When I read Dylan Thomas, Seamus Heaney, William Butler Yeats and other masters of Welsh and Irish verse, I am full of awe (even if not complete understanding) of what they write and how they write. I am profoundly aware that I could never hope to emulate any, even minute, aspect of their genius, but they do provide me with inspiration. Around 2004, therefore, I started to compose some poems, initially solely for my own benefit.

Many of the poems I have written in the succeeding decade have arisen during journeys that I and my wife Peggy (who also has a Celtic background) have made throughout the world. Most trips had a professional basis but we used them to visit wonderful, sometimes exotic and nearly always captivating places. During the decade, however, we noted changes taking place around us that seemed to call out for some commentary, or perhaps just some passing observation. It is these changes that I have endeavoured to capture in my poems.

Towards the end of 2014, I decided to compile the poems into a volume, which I have entitled 'A Decade of Transition'. Although there are some recurring themes, and indeed some recurring locations, the poems are set out chronologically, perhaps with an eye to my own changing perceptions. During this time, our geographical base changed, involving transitions from Northern Europe (Cheshire and Brussels) to the USA (North Carolina) and to South Africa (Franschhoek, Western Cape). I appreciate that it is not normal in a collection of poems to give explanations of what each poem is about, but I thought a few sentences would be helpful to put them into the context of Peggy and my travels and observations.

CONTENTS

Trying to do something different later in life is not trivial. In my case, ignoring long-held traditional views and habits in scientific methodology and thinking, and adopting a new form of communication and writing style was a challenge. As with everything I have done over many years, this would not have been possible without the encouragement, support and practical help of my wife Peggy. She has always been a close partner in all of our professional activities, and her influence on my scientific writing, editing and speaking has been profound. She immediately recognized that the writing of poetry had to be my work and my work alone, so she patiently waited while I spent hours in the evenings, often sitting outside our house or hotel with a glass of wine, and slowly put together or reshaped the words and lines that form this compilation. I am tremendously grateful to Peggy for this. But more than support and patience, my interest in poetry needed practical encouragement, and Peggy arranged several poetry readings in Winston Salem North Carolina as well as the inaugural Café Poétique in Franschhoek, South Africa. She was also fully involved in the publishing of this book, undertaken by ourselves and the wonderful design team of Design for development (D4D) in Cape Town. As the title states, this project has taken a decade; it has been both different and exciting and I record here my appreciation for everything
Peggy has contributed.

David Williams
Franschhoek, South Africa
March 2016

MALDIVIAN HOPE

Not long before the powerful tsunami wreaked havoc in South-east Asia and the Indian Ocean, we visited the Maldives, a very long archipelago to the south west of India. Discussions of climate change and global warming were taking place around the world, of course, but little was being done. Staying on an island whose highest point was only just above the waterline emphasized the fragile nature of the land-sea interface.

Infinity by two metres
Depending on the time of day and month
And the vagaries of the Indian Ocean
Elliptical shards of coral sand
Living in the fear
That heralds the first nation to go asunder
As the big men trade their targets
And the glaciers feed the hungry seas

It was not always thus

These seas, and the remorseless energy of their waves
Have long been known to man, and indeed warmly embraced
As they discriminate this earth from the planetary aridness elsewhere
The oceans and rivers breathe life into the land they touch

It could have always been thus

Yet, that touch can, and should be, the caress of the lover
As in Venice, or Capri or gay Paris
Or even the harbours of Sydney or Casablanca
Yet the wilds of Cape Cod or Galway Bay

But it will not always be thus

Those who live by the sea know they may die by the sea
And the price they pay may be profound
A murderous blow not a caress
The cruel sea will someday win

Maldives
January 2004

UNCHAINED TETHERS

Several years before what became known as the Arab Spring we paid our second visit to Morocco. Even within the few years since the last time we were there, it was possible to sense a change in the people; there was a new, welcomed, monarch, but tension was in the air. They were scared and excited, arrogant and frightened, all at the same time.

Metallic vectors from the north
Exchange old eyes for heavy purses
Fearsome young hopefuls drawn
Towards the neo-promised land

The blend of doubt and pride
Yields uncertainty at their door
The strands of time already blur
The lessons gone and those to come

Which way does the minaret face
Can Mecca still be seen through the Atlas peaks
Did the French and the Jews leave the Berber untouched
Can the Souk, the Medina, the Kasbah survive

The flux of microwave, Mercedes and jazz
The loss of the lifelines of their future
Muezzin and mobile, discordant, compete
The old lute is tethered to the amp

A purchase in the Souk consummated by card
Guides already the Euro demand
Clothes of Gucci or labelled Zinedine
Mask faded kaftan and dull djellaba

Marrakech, Morocco
March 2004

WARD C

Hospitals are rarely bright and beautiful places, as worried patients, families and friends mix with earnest professionals doing their best for those in their care. I have a genetic condition that is not at all troublesome, as long as I have five or six phlebotomies every year, where a volume of blood, and the excess iron it contains, is removed from my body and thrown away. My condition thus requires me to attend a hospital, wherever in the world we are, for this procedure, which is usually done in the cancer ward – since that is where haematologists largely work and where the nurses have the skills to painlessly get into the veins. So I am treated in a ward surrounded by patients with the most serious of conditions.

I sit on a bed
Not unhealthy but in palliative care
Around me, the smiling dying
Taking transfusions and chemos
Like infants at the breast
Wide-eyed, safe at the succour
Embraced by the fleshy but sexless carers
Who leave their own problems at the door
And administer to, and talk to, and
Engage with those who do not know
What tomorrow will bring

I do

I read the news while the blood drips out
The technical leak that keeps me healthy
While the murderous leash of cancer
Remorselessly expunges hope from some
In their anaemic, leukemic state

Chester, England
April 2004

AN INDIAN SUMMER

Taking time off from a lecture tour of India, we visit Rajasthan, from the Taj Mahal to the Pink City of Jaipur. The contrasts of poverty and splendour are profound; so too are the expectations of life.

In utter dysenteric squalor
His life emerged and engaged,
Poorly nourished breasts gave little succour
His scraps came from the infectious floor
No dinner table but a flourish of hands
Drawing rice from the pot
Mixed with the detritus of life
That floated by on that Rajasthani day

They shared three rooms
Four generations and their cattle, of equal stature
Piously claiming their space in quiet order
Seasonal sun drove away the remnants of the monsoon disorder
As rancid, excreta-infected mud gave way
To putrid, dust-embedded stone
Dwellings merged seamlessly with the voluminous waste
That was home to the lesser swine and untouchables

But the landscape was a scene of laughter and play and learning
No matter the squalor, the smiles pervaded all
The school books proudly raised themselves above the dirt
And no doctors were needed to soothe tainted throats

No shouts, no screams from the shoeless infants
As they effortlessly crossed the burning rocky street
No plaintiff cries
And never a tear to be seen

Their long since departed and distant cousins
Had been born to expatriated forebears
Now ensconced for a few generations in a brave new world
Thoroughly entrenched in the opposite diameter
Where natural immunity is redundant through lack of work
Endlessly supported by needled vaccines,
No dysentery, malaria, cholera or the poxes
Just fatness and arrogance fed by parental pride

Life misses nothing, no chances are lost
Hardware and software surround them with sounds
Learning a given, though not by the book
Rather by screens where truth and fantasy co-exist
They should be the content ones, possessive of everything
But petulance displaces laughter when instance is not there
Teeth are bared in anger not smiles
Tears and tantrums pervade all

Who are the fortunate
Whose integrated contentment is the best
Do we have to make progress
At the expense of humility?

Rajasthan, India
December 2004

CHATTRA SAGAR

*On that same journey in India, we find a remarkable village, with a tented
hotel on the shores of a reservoir, and centuries-old images.*

At its southern door, the Pink City turns a shade of grey
Fuelled by the diesel that pervades and persuades
The never-ending line of polluting vectors of trade
On the incomplete superhighway to Mumbai, and beyond
Overloaded with manifest, under-endowed with sense
The modern-day pretenders to Genghis Khan
See the challenge of six lanes stretching unfettered to eternity
With no comprehension of the carnage that unbridled inertia will bring.

But that is tomorrow; today gives a chance
To deviate, to digress, to escape from the chaos
Long before Udaipur, west towards Jodhpur and the Aravali hills
And Nimaj
The dusty, soft-sanded road, brightened by the sari-clad backs in green fields
Gives only a hint of what is over the near horizon
The first water of any form to be seen this day
Collects itself in splendour, under Chattra Sagar

A reservoir of tranquillity, a foyer of calm
Derived straight from the water-colour masterpiece
Subtle land hues of green, yellow and ochre
Join the heavenly blue to the bird-speckled watery haven
For rising above the western edge
Is a ridge, a buttress against incivility
On which the generous share their oasis
With those fortunate to have escaped the Rajasthani day

An oasis in an ocean of impatience
Where the speed of light perceptibly slows
The interlude between sunset and moonrise
Both deliciously captured on that ridge
Rids for a moment the shards of life
Replacing them with the soothed edges of serenity
The delicate heron on the opposite shore
Looks up and smiles at Chattra Sagar

Rajasthan, India
December 2004

MENDING THE BROKEN HEART

On our first extensive visit to South Africa, where our work brings us into contact with the world famous Groote Schuur hospital of Cape Town, we had some time to contemplate the juxtaposition of poetry and medicine. The complexity but fragility of the heart would become my focus of attention for the next decade.

He can live forever in the persistent but euphemistic vegetative state
Death does not come easily to the ailing brain,
Traumatic disturbance of the spine kills feeling, but not life,
Cirrhosis takes years to wither the final stages of gin
Loss of hearing and vision inconvenience but do not fatally maim
But missing a single heartbeat is the beginning of the end, a quick ending of life

That degenerate brain keeps the heart alive
Often giving perverse succour where it is no longer respected
You have to mend a broken heart quickly
Since it strokes the genius and then the life out of the white matter above,

A mass of muscle, a bundle of nerves,
Shimmering, pulsating, the essence of life,
Architectural similes, of arches, atria, portals and septa
Activities fundamental for living, rhythm, pulse, beat,
Its deficiencies initiate the decline, dissent and incipient death,
Murmur, attack, occlusion, clot,
The adjectives and nouns of the incompetent and dying

A heart, broken, forever denied the power of recovery
The epitome of irrecoverable traumatic decline
Heart-wrenching, tearing, stopping phenomena,
No soothing words, no emollient of help.

Why has God ordained it thus, that the
Incompetent and incontinent live forever
But the transient infarct in the life and soul of the party
Kills both instantly?

Can this change, can the glue be found to mend the broken heart?
Not the machine to replace it; that is no answer,
A technical chance for the few, to be sure, but
Of no affordable value to the hearts of the many.

No, the death of the heart, which brings death to the soul, starts with the death of
some cells,
The primordial cells of the pulsating beat
Can we bring them back to life, can we regenerate
The few, can we persuade the body
To heal itself, in that moment of time,
In that deliciously delicate of all places,
Through that molecular glue of *cellule souche*?

Of course we can,
With care, humility, and no heroics.

Franschhoek, South Africa
February 2005

QUANTUM DOT

Medical technology is increasingly becoming reliant on nanotechnology,
with all the uncertainties that it brings.

Oh, quantum dot
Where art thou
I can't see you
But I know you're there

Aren't you?

Cheshire, England
July 2005

LIVERPOOL STREET BLUES

*The heads of state of those countries bidding for the Summer Olympics
of 2012 met in Singapore to hear the committee's decision. Among them was
the Prime Minister of the UK, intent on pressing the London case. No sooner
had he returned to that city, than terrorists' actions shattered euphoria and
many lives.*

*(With grateful acknowledgement to the Beatles for some of their lines, which
I have adapted.)*

———————

The man, centre stage
Shaken but visibly stirred
Is a pale shadow of yesterday
Yesterday

All his troubles seemed so far away.

A victory of Trafalgar proportions
Away in the Far East, with Olympics secured,
And now, in sombre mood,
With an effete and defeated French emperor
Standing over his shoulder
Wondering what it would be like
To win and lose a city in a day
Just imagine.

Imagine there's no hell
It's not easy when you try
Those still interred underground

Go down, down, down
And in the distance emerges the Styx
Only before seen in nightmares
Hades takes over from the Angel
The Cross moves from Kings to the Devil

All those lonely people
Where do they all go now?
A long and winding road
For lonely dying people

Oh, for sunshine on a cloudy day
Please, don't take our sunshine away

But Tony, don't carry the world on your shoulder
The yellow rose of Texas wants to hold your hand
Help him if you can and
Take a sad day and make it better

Hey dudes, don't let us down
Turn on your axis of evil
Bring home your purveyors of shock and awe
Remember those who were wiser than thou
The evil that men do lives after them
The good is oft interred in their bones
It's now or never for you
As the souls go marching on

Liverpool, England,
July 2005

FROM KYOTO
TO NEW ORLEANS

The power of Hurricane Katrina needs no explanation.

————————————

The sunny side of the street is gone, perhaps forever
They no longer pass by saying how do you do
The blues have lost their shades downtown
As New Orleans becomes the Baghdad, the Bosnia, the Beirut of Black America

Katrina, a Russian goddess just made for Wimbledon
Revealed her true identity skirting round Florida
Twisting, teasing, tantalising, attracting the eye
Of a storm of record Louisiana dimensions

It was a long time coming, but it arrived in style
The inevitable destructive swing of a mighty tail
Colliding with the personification of an underbelly
Spilling out the entrails of a society
Already below the poverty line, now literally drowning
In the excrement of neglect

The French had no right to quarter here
Levees were no match for the copied dykes
Two centuries of misguided hope
Masked the engineered alarm
As defences inferior to those of Amsterdam and Venice
Crumbled under forces Europe never knew

Gravity determined the inevitable, the lake flowed downhill
Just a metre or so sufficient
To submerge and drown cats and immobile people
Retrograde police movements, met by the influx of carpetbaggers and worse
Old folks and their care-homes deserted and rent asunder
Survival instincts clashing with opportunistic crime

The world's only superpower
Now powerless before nature's anger
How dare you ignore the warnings
How dare you sacrifice the world
To the avarice of the billionaire cabinet
How can you be born again
Whilst forsaking Kyoto's umbilicus
Using it to strangle the underclass

Cheshire, England
September 2005

THE MARSHES OF PUDONG

Our first experience of China came in 2005: Shanghai, a city of old European concessions, now alive with power and money, especially on the Pudong side of the Huangpu River.

Asia in turmoil, underground and above
The earth moving beneath the collective feet
As tsunami and Kashmiri earthquake shock stability
Tremors unnerve warlords over the region
Iraq has elections, dictatorship quivers
Gaza evacuates, a defensive attack
Iran threatens and Chechnya still exists
While avian flu poses airborne destruction to the living world

Now the streets of Pudong shudder the most vibrantly
With excitement and knee-trembling fear
Six hundred years after the first Ming throne
Wrested global monopoly
Suppressing the Khans, Genghis and Kublai, and other Moghul lords
Only to succumb to the introversion and insecurity endemic in the region
Shanghai and Beijing have now risen, Phoenix-like
From the ashes of the Cultural Revolution

The Huangpu, the present day Thames, Seine, Danube and Hudson
The right bank of the east eclipsing the left bank of the west
Wall Street and the Square Mile signal they are waking, as giants are supposed to do
But the Gullivers are held by the ties of the Lilliputian minnows
From street-side trading to the virtual floor
Rings are being run around the foreigners
Lulled by the ubiquitous Starbucks and fast food
Stunned by the energy and fast thinking

Pudong was a marsh, a wasteland, until late
While Paris, London and Berlin sought supremacy in Europe
The marshes recovered and reclaimed land
To dwarf Canary Wharf
To kill the Footsie and CAC
China will own us, control us
Play games with us, laugh at us
As the marshes of Pudong stand aloft

Shanghai, China
October 2005

A MINOR REARRANGEMENT

We had been in Phuket, Thailand for a vacation some years previously. A year after the Asian tsunami, which brought so much damage to this part of the world, we returned.

The sand is the same
So is the water, greyish blue, wavy
Unloading flotsam on the Andaman shore
Clouds tumble by, high in the sky
Like they always have
Paying no attention to their fuzzy shadows below

Trees still stand, a little more weathered perhaps
Early morning fisherman set their nets
Less in number, more in fear
Feral dogs with no homes of their own
No beachcomber's scraps for survival
The same but different

The palm-thatched roofs are no longer there
Timbered shanties gone forever
A wall here, toppled beams there
Ghostly remnants of backpackers' havens
Empty chairs and empty tables
Mangled, deserted and forlorn

One year ago, the mighty ocean spoke
Responding to the growling, quaking earth
A single transient devastating surge
That tore apart those who collectively
Lived down by the sea
And then returned to normal

The same sand and the same ocean
Rearranged rocks on a devastated land

Phuket, Thailand
December 2005

THE UGLY WARTHOG

*My first poem about an African safari, but the action took place
as we landed at the lodge's airstrip.*

The runt of the litter
Had no sense and no speed
To get out of the way

The sun had warmed the strip
A family enjoying the heat
The plane approached, circled
Enticing the animals away
Mother ran, siblings ran
But Dunlop was too slow

A wheel, with Dunlop tyres
Glanced the then unnamed cub
Who now acquired a name and a limp

The airstrip boss
Took pity, amazingly
Gave succour to the injured
Milk from the bottle
A mat on the floor
Some hope to get better

But warthogs don't belong
To bricks and wood
They're not renowned
For reciprocating care
Preferring to mess up the place
He had to go

Now here is the rub
What is most delicious
For the waiting wild dog
Hyena, cheetah or even lion
A tasty four-legged steak
That has not learnt to run or fight

Rock and hard place, nowhere to hide
Dunlop wanders off
Into his own sunset

Phinda Lodge, KwaZulu-Natal, South Africa
March 2006

THE LEOPARD
AND THE LOOKING GLASS

We saw her at sundown
Teaching her cub how to score
The hyena said 'no I am the king
Of the dead, it's mine now'
The cub was brave
But the mother wise
And they let the buck be dragged
Away from them and their hunger

Next morning at dawn
We saw her again
Still hungry and forlorn
Has to look for something new
But nothing was there
As the heat of the day
Drove even the vermin underground
Until she saw the light

In the distance, the lodge of humans
Those arrogant apes
With their infernal machines
That torture us
Just like they cannot be seen

They watch us laugh at us
Capture us through their lenses
They are there every way we turn

At their temporary home
Having graced us with their presence
Evening and morn
Watching us kill and copulate
They return for rest
Our food, the antelope, the bok
Now spiced and turned
In their ovens of fire

They think they are safe
No fence no guards
Just the feeling that the smell
Of dominant man will keep us away
Here they are
By their own waterhole
Escaping the heat
As if they owned all

The leopard silently climbs
The man rests his eyes
It crouches on the deck
He senses the change
It rises to the pool
He opens his eyes
They look at each other
A world apart through the glass

Singita Lodge, Kruger National Park, South Africa
March 2007

THE TIANANMEN SHROUD

Back to China and the contrast that Beijing, with its historical and political power, has to offer, compared to Shanghai, with its financial prowess.

Night is not quite finished
A few hours before, we rode rickshaws
Through the descending rubble of the Beijing backstreets
Yards from the teahouses of upper class China, a million miles from their affluence
A jaunt back to the opulent international hotel
From the theatre of acrobats, kung fu, mime and changing masks

Powerful young men pushed or pedalled along
An illegal route skirting Tiananmen Square
More than a match for the Marrakech Souk or the Delhi of old
Surprising and frightening rats and lovers alike
Both exposing their raw needs of the night
As overground and underground merged with olfactory collusion.

The Olympics are coming, two years away but only one side of the city is on show
The other three sides of the square of life
Yet to expire and rebuild in their image of the new future
One Dream, one World, one Side

An interlude, an injection of wine, a few hours sleep
Dawn is ready to arrive, if it only could
The modern Beijing will not accede
Full moon demure, behind the Chinese walls of fog and low flying cloud
What do they want us to see, what remains hidden
Do they dare to include deity in their command?

We walk by ourselves in an eerie start
Wondering why we are alone on this day
Through the silence of the mist
Several thousand now surround us, on the edge
Prevented by the uniforms from entering The Square
The students of yesterday
Now carrying their children not their hopes on their shoulders
The Imperial Guard emerges, in silence apart from their goose step sounds
Flag-waving children mute, red and blue sirens of the police flash but do not chime
The military band, under the Chairman's gaze, musically raises the red flag
Dawn magically arises above the haze
As those on the ground still wait
For enlightenment, as the steps re-cross the road from whence they came
The people go about their business, dropping the new red warrants in the gutter
To hustle unheard-of yuan
In the new Beijing Day

Beijing, China
October 2008

A LONG TRAIN WEAVES SLOWLY THROUGH THE KANSAS CITY NIGHT

The Midwest does not connote hedonism or even excitement. Kansas City is not a favourite destination, even for just one night in a downtown hotel, but where better to relive some long-forgotten dreams?

(The image is of a Dylan Lewis sculpture, with acknowledgement to The Dylan Lewis Sculpture Garden, Stellenbosch)

Immediately deep sleep
Then lighter
Then deeper again
The past returns
As always in distorted form
Turn over, and again and again
Troubled sleep is no friend
Everything moving, coming and going
Mostly coming, towards you
You're in the way, whatever you do
Wherever you turn, you're in the way
The trucks, the planes, the cycles, the runners

You're always in their way
People you once knew
Push you into their way
Converging on you
But keeping you asleep, just,
Until you go deeper and quieter again

Now comes the train
Not the lyrical Chattanooga or San Fernando
But the fearful, frightful freight
Miles between engine and caboose
Of lumber, coal, steel and grain
No escaping this
You are right in the way
Petrified between rails unable to move

The deadly concoction
Of sound and silence
Across the plains it came
Weaving slowly downtown
A mile from the hotel bed
Where sleep had been possible
Troubled, but now uncertain
The haunting whistle
Announcing arrival in the city
What is it? I must be in the way
No, it's all right, the silence of midnight
Lulls you back into a fitful sleep

The next crossing, more screeching
Again the brain responds
Fear and partial awakening
Trembling, shivering in the heat
Prayers demand silence
Which announces itself eerily
The nerves await the next bend
Rumble after rumble
Minutes, maybe hours churn by
Awake, fear; asleep fear
Where is the difference?
The border between reality and nowhere is so small

The long train wanders by
Am I the only one to be troubled
To vacillate among the 'wake and the dead
As it shunts forward
Leaving the trail of shattered thought
Departing the city, to Chicago and beyond
Awaiting the sunrise and the real awakening
Distant thoughts of what went by
Live again till the next dream train

Kansas City, Missouri, USA
June 2010

VUVUZELA, MANDELA

The soccer world cup comes to South Africa, more remembered by the sounds than the sport. Two poems.

———————

Vuvuzela
Mandela
One pitch cacophony
Piercing decibels
One nation's symphony
Of forgiven cells
Joyous bellicose sounds
Ephemeral bafana fun
God's heaven bound
Invictus' work done
A rainbow of noise and colour
Starts and ends as one

Cape Town, South Africa
December 2010

A BEAUTIFUL GAME DIES

Over-rated, overpaid prima donnas
In their own small town back home
Collectively fail on the world stage
As form, desire, pride forsake them
Under the glare of expectation
In the wondrous new stadia of hope

Zuma stands proud
As his country accepts the challenge
He stands yawning
As he watches cheats and fairies
Who pout and cry and feign
The derision descends on feebleness and pathos

Could Cape Town, Durban and Jo'burg
Deliver at the apogee of the game?
Could Xhosa, Zulu and Afrikaans
Join as one nation?
Of course they could, and did
At the graveside of the beautiful game

Cape Town, South Africa
December 2010

THE BLUES, BUT NO JAZZ

*No explanation is needed here, as the world is still reeling from
financial stupidity, incompetence and corruption.*

No one sings
Oh, what a beautiful morning
Anymore
No folks pass you by
Saying how do you do
All saying I love you
Anymore
The words and news of today
Are all so different
Vocabulary is of austerity, foreclosure
Disabled and bankrupt
Regulation and deregulation
Fiscal prudence or irresponsibility
Who knows, where is common sense

The reality is
Oiled cormorants on Louisiana beaches
IEDs mangle NATO peacekeepers
Volcanoes close airspace
Unseasonable snows close groundspace
Gunmen amok globally
Politicians always in the trough
Financiers defy gravity
Sports decision-makers join in
We do not need G20s and economists to change us
We need Monk, Fitzgerald, Gillespie, Humph and Armstrong
And some Amazing Grace would help

North Carolina, USA
April 2011

THE COLD HEAT OF NANOSCIENCE

Back to some science, and nanotechnology again, where there is a great deal of confusion and debate about the promise and dangers of man's exploitation of the nanoscale. One of the world's epicentres of nanotechnology is in China.

An organism of massive dimension
Where febrile peripheral matrices
Are overcome by urban cellular fusion
To develop chaotic debris
Within their nuclei
Party-fed vectors
Homecoming super-idols
Change the DNA
Rapidly evolving societal nature
Following Huxley, Verne, Orwell
Presenting a new Da Vinci nanocode

With a Feynman approach
In a far-from-primeval swamp
Assembly at the nanolevel
Builds nucleic acid engines
Intended to power regeneration
Of hearts and minds, even souls

The swamp changes to a lake
And lakes metaphorically collect
As the nodes of Jiangsu
Close to the aorta of the organism
Powerfully beating to the intensity
The white heat of yesterday's technology
Transfers to the cold fusion of Suzhou

Suzhou, China
May 2011

REVENGE FOR INVICTUS

There is only one sport that is worthy of attention and that is rugby union. The power of the game facilitated the end of apartheid in South Africa, demonstratedin the film 'Invictus'. The rugby world cup took place in New Zealand in 2011.

The land of the long white cloud
Soaring eagles and spring-like deer
Force the quaking fear
Over the gain line of hope and pride
In empathy, a tsunami from the North
Joins the ruck and the mall of the South

The RWC, for short, is here
Exchange for the moment
Brute power of the Lions game
For the nose-touching Maori welcome
Earth-shattering noise of the Celts
Drowns the peace of Kiwi and Auk

The passion of the daffodils
And the leaves of the Shamrock
Put the mighty nations to shame
Red roses and blossoms fall short
Azzurri's scrum collapses
Jocks meet their nemesis in Malvinas
England have Georgia on their mind
Petit Tonga blow away the French

Wallabies out-jumped by Leprechauns
From the high veld of Gauteng
To the valleys of Rhondda
Malone in Dublin
Matilda down-under
Wales wins the anthems
All Blacks the haka
Hospitality for some, hospital-passes for others
Rugby's welcome to ferocity

In the final dying days
Sam's card the colour of his shirt
Leaks tears in the valleys
Leaves tous noir contre les Bleus
A nation saved by a point
The cup of world's rugby over-floweth

Wellington, New Zealand
November 2011

PLEASE DO GO GENTLY

Dylan Thomas famously wrote about his father's decline and suggested that he should not become milder as he faded away. Some may differ when they witness such fading.

A strong father
Always with his own way
Slips slowly into the soft eventide
A rebellious son, unused to this surrender
Delivers, epically, do not go gentle into that good night

Angry young men vitalize
Angry old men embarrass
Rational disagreement
Even flowing with invective
Can enrich the active debate

But when confused febrile defensive veterans
Effuse accumulated bile
Into any listening ear
Respect is the loser
There's not one winner
A good life becomes soiled
The last memories tainted
The marathon runner falls over
His mouth in the last mile
Please do go gently into that good night

Winston-Salem, North Carolina, USA
May 2011

ODE TO GRAYLYN

A brief story about a visiting cat, never seen by us before, who chose our house as his last resting place. We called the cat 'Graylyn'.

Stray, gray
Death a heart beat away
Just here to say
Can't stay
Another day
Please, with passion, lay
Me down, and say
He was good, but lost his way
In the dying days of May.

Winston-Salem, North Carolina, USA
June 2011

KAZAKHSTAN CROSSROADS

*A short visit to Kazakhstan, to give some lectures, just before the long,
hard winter set in, revealed just how far this former Soviet country,
in the Steppes of Asia, has come since independence, but raised questions
about contrasts between old habits and oil-fuelled progress.*

Between Nepal and the North Pole
Midway Moscow and Mongolia
Shaped by old mosque domes
Oiled by new moguls' wells
Where Russian rockets reached for rendezvous
And Soviet steppes still stand
A Dubai without sun, Doha its sheiks
Bright seeds of Astana sprout tall

Smooth young faces vie with gnarled age
Imported fashion edges cossack furs
Uncertain snow now pushed aside
Not allowed to dampen the fever
Feel the pulse of the Eurasian heart
New blood and oil course through the veins
Mixing together in the vortex of life

Twenty years free of the Kremlin
Not quite yet of the age of maturity
A crossroads of Clapton dimensions

Waiting to see the signs
Let it grow, let it grow
Where young minds yearn and blossom
Emerging from the long Siberian night

Astana, Kazakhstan
November 2011

THE WELL OF XI'AN

The discovery of the Terracota Warriers in Xi'an, China transformed
this ancient city to being the host of a world-class museum.

In the centre of the fog-shrouded city
The buildings do not scrape the sky
So elegantly as in Beijing
Nor so daringly as Shanghai
The attention focuses instead
To the earth, down a few meters

A humble farmer looking for water
Found how terra firma
Had been changed to terra cotta
By the mighty Qin

Preparing for his heavenly journey
Supported by a cast of warriors
Cherubs and their horses
Virgins and their minders

Having unified the country taking his own name
He departed in a tomb enriched beyond dreams
Now awed by the Chinese multitude
Wondering where their own dynasty leads

Xi'an, China
April 2013

ORCHIDS LOST IN CONGRESS

*Several poems have their origins in contemporary politics
and need little explanation.*

———————————

Those who say
I will only say
What I think
Are doomed to end their days
With no-one at their graves
Save others who dance on the brink

The art of diplomacy
Getting your way with magnanimity
Giving away what not matters
Generosity that deceives to flatter
But keeping behind the brick
To snuff out the candle's wick

Tea parties are great
For those under eight
Fun, no responsibility
Intellectual infidelity
No compassion from me
'Case it sets you free

*North Carolina, USA
September 2013*

THE END
OF POLITICAL VISION

Presidential pretenders
Spend months and fortunes
Persuading a credulous populace
That their vision will reunite America

One hundred days they gave JFK
That mantra has strayed
No longer a honeymoon for the victor
Minimal post-partum period when the womb is safe
After which it is ripe for invasion
Raped by engorged losers
Usurping the vision
That has gone before

Instead of using the votes he has won
He starts counting those he has lost
Less than two years to the mid-terms
Three to the primaries
Four to the next vote
Scores have to be settled
Factions coveted
Lobbyists appeased

Campaign pledges ignored
Opportunistic positions adopted
Reversing direction at ease
Policies are not foreign
Nor climate, nor health nor fiscal
Only who will vote for me next time
What do I have to pay
And to whom to make it so

North Carolina, USA
September 2013

LOST MEMORIES AT THE TABLE

*Table Mountain in Cape Town is a wonderful sight, especially on
a beautiful spring evening, sitting on the Waterfront; but the whispery
clouds that form on the table summon some other ideas.*

———————

I rest in Bascule
Intent on slowing the pace of my brain cells
For a leisurely evening
Of thoughtful solitude
Before flying the Cape

Over the brim of a Neil Ellis
The cleanest of tables
Massive flat ear to the east of Lion's Head
Clear, as the sun diminishes its influence
A mighty proud dominance
Of all around
Resembling a forehead of aged wisdom

From the left, a wisp of white
And maybe doubt
As the clarity is threatened
By threads and yarns of cloud
That forehead recedes
Taken over by a silver lining
As the cloth is draped
Over the table

The granite head
So eminent before
Quakes a little in uncertainty
The grey matter bubbles along with our champagne

Behind me
The nubile waterfront
Uncouthly brings on the night
Raucous hedonism
Reminds us of yesterday
As the old man above
Is enveloped in uncertainty
Not knowing where he is
No memory of what went before

Cape Town, South Africa
November 2013

DARKNESS AND LIGHTNESS FROM THE PAST: DE LA BELGIQUE À L'AFRIQUE DU SUD

I wrote a few poems for our premier Café Poétique, held in Franshhoek, South Africa in 2014. I have hosted a few Café Scientifiques around the world, including one in Franschhoek a few years earlier in which we described our work with children suffering from rheumatic heart disease. We decided that it was appropriate now to turn our attention to poetry; the event was called 'The Heart of Lightness'.

He saw the Congo, a mighty river
As an immense snake, uncoiled
With its head in the ocean
A body slithering
The tail lost in the depths of Africa
Conrad's heart of darkness

Masking the Belgian route of ivory
Sinister on the left, righteous on the other side
Untamed through the then undemocratic republic
A reptilian watercourse
Of Amazonian dimensions
The dark bleeding heart of Africa

Hearts of old people are strong
Some too strong for their ailing brain
Maybe they should give up earlier

Hearts of young people are fragile
Yes, in a foolish romantic way
But more profoundly in disease-ridden shacks
Where there are no watercourses
Even today
Of any dimension

Conrad wasn't to know
Where the really dark hearts were
They are here, further south
We have to prevent the massacre
Of young hearts and lives
Bringing much more lightness to the Cape

Cape Franschhoek, South Africa
February 2014

DARKNESS AND LIGHTNESS FROM THE PRESENT: MUSIQUE À STELLENBOSCH

Oude Libertas
A heart-shaped amphitheatre
Of strings
A Soweto quartet
And a flamenco duet flourishing from the Cape
Lightness grew amidst the darkening skies of even'

Black on white
Afrikaans and Xhosa
Young and older
History and anticipation

Serious undertones but refreshing notes
Across the immense divide
Just twenty years on
Could I believe what I saw
In Stellenbosch?
Yes I could, and did
And they finaled
With the Madiba Jive
Could you ask for more enlightenment in your heart?

Cape Franschhoek, South Africa
February 2014

THE LIGHTNESS OF MY FATHERS

My first memory was Llandrindod
Between Machynlleth and Llanidloes
Where the best place names
Have no vowels
Between 4Ls, 2Ds and 5Ys
The pubs had no beer on Sundays
Because we were dry, except of humour
And we were in the chapel all day anyway
From Llywelyn ap Gruffydd to Catherine Zeta Jones
St David to Burton and Terfel
Jones and Williams and Davies alike
We could sing and act and play rugby
Like no-one before or since
All the coal came from us
And a little gold
Most of it around Peggy's neck now
There was so little
We had dragons before the Chinese
Pretty daffodils in top hats

Where could romance start
If not in Betws-y-Coed, Bryn Mawr and Aberystwyth?
How Green Was My Valley
You may well ask

Cape Franschhoek, South Africa
February 2014

THE LOVER'S GAZE

Back on safari, we had a close encounter with a massive male elephant.

____

He's in musth
I must
Get out of this place

Not a pretty sight
An elephant a yard away
Urine effusing
From every orifice

His eyes meet mine
He knows no fear
Trunk assailing
Mouth agape
Acacias uprooted
The land tremors

Don't worry, says tracker Shoes
Nervously edging back into his seat
Steve rests his hands
Nonchalantly on his rifle
Don't be scared they all say
Seen it many times before

Hey, my first one
Swallow hard, look straight back
No difference, nothing to swallow
Saliva deserted minutes ago

But they're right, and relieved
Not interested in inconsequential me
Just in his lover
On the other side of the track

Cape Franschhoek, South Africa
February 2014

RENDEZVOUS

This poem is inspired by the sound of the Cape Eagle Owl.

At the bedside you
Pray, or maybe suggest
That the feral dogs
Or those abandoned
Do not set
A cacophonous cascade
Of barking
That keeps all awake
At night

This time it is good
No noise at all until four
Then the most wonderful of sounds
Dogs clearly asleep
A Cape Eagle Owl
On our roof

Talking to a mate
A mile away
Replies come back softly
Our friend gets louder
Mice and young guineafowl
Seek shelter
But the cross-talk gets sweeter
Faster and softer
They arrange a rendezvous
In a copse at dawn

Cape Franschhoek, South Africa
March 2014

THE FINISHING LINE

Back in the USA, the fragility of the ageing population becomes more evident by the day.

———————

There is grey matter and white matter
White fat and brown fat
Red cells and white cells
Shouldn't they all cross the finish line
Together, when we go

No, they take it in turns
Some bone cells today
You walk a little less
Retinal cells tomorrow
We see a little less
Arteries blocking slowly
Makes breathing laboured
Are we close to that line
No, not yet

A disc slips one way
Pinching a nerve as it goes
A sphincter gets looser
No one wants to know

Why can't they go at once
So we prepare for our maker
In one healthy piece
Then painlessly say goodbye

Because the brain and the heart
Do not agree with each other
Don't work together, never did
Mind and matter
Body and soul
Compete to see which lasts longer

The brain usually gives up first
Leaving the heart pounding away
At that door, unable
Unwilling to understand
That all else has passed the line

North Carolina, USA
April 2014

CHILD'S PLAY

I find it difficult to write poetically about science; it is possible to write some good lines but to retain meaning is not easy. This poem is about stem cells, describing them in terms and objects that should be familiar, especially to those who live in our area.

———————

Take a clear sandwich bag
From Trader Joe's
Place inside a mesh of linguine
Cooked to softly perfection in Toscana
Surround by vanilla jello
From Harris Teeter
Mix in a concoction of drugs
Prescription serviced by CWS
Add health supplements
Wisely obtained at Whole Foods
Delicately place in the middle, one soft egg yolk
Infuse with vitamin pills
Sourced carefully online

Now, since this is child's play
Get little, very little, candies
From Walgreens
Place them in the saved egg white
And paste this on the
Outside of the bag
Conjure up some Atala magic
Infuse energy
Just a little oxygen
It gets smaller and smaller
The mimicry of life
In fact, the origin of the species
The cellular stem of living

Winston-Salem, North Carolina, USA
April 2014

MILLENNIA OF STEALTH

Still with biology and medicine, and a further emphasis on nanoscience,
where it is possible to combine nanoparticles and drugs so the body's normal
defence mechanisms are fooled and the drug gets to its target more easily.

———————

Both Virgil and Homer
Recounted the story of Troy
Epic or myth is not certain
But the plan was masterful

For many a long day the Greeks had pressed
Yet could not enter nor vanquish
The Trojan people or their army
Which festered like a tumour in the pride of the invaders

So they presented a horse
Now the eponymous equine stealth
A massive wooden reparation
For the victors inside the city
From the departing losers
Who made to go home
Fooling most, though not all,
That their warriors were effete and gone

But inside the wooden animal
Were a clutch of the not-so-wooden elite
Of the erstwhile invaders
Who with surprise and speed
Rendered the celebrating victors

Some lethal targeted blows
Unnerving the defensive structure
When least expected

Millennia on
And still not fully certain
Stealth is with us again
Nanoscopic not monolithic
The little Troys are now cancers
Evasive cells that repulse many an attack
Through defences that mutate
Capable of avoiding the spears of chemical drugs

Their walls and membranes so powerful
That few lethal molecules can pass
Turning their attention to weaker parts of the host
In hair follicles and intestines
The chemo-infantry have to stand aside
And give way to special agents
Trained to befriend the guards at the gate
Slipping their cocktail between arms and legs into the lair

Antibody targeted, magnetically guided
The minute nanocreatures
Attack the enemy
Leaving aside workers, straight for the queen
Where they deliver their toxic payload
Like the elite Grecian swordsmen
Once inside the malignant enemy
No defence survives

North Carolina, USA
April 2014

A DAY IN THE LIFE OF HUNGER

Hunger is pervasive. We see evidence of hunger and attempts to ameliorate it most places we go, including both Winston-Salem and Cape Town.

———————

The neighbourhood cat
Wanders up again
Looking for food
Nothing there, nothing lost

A cockroach slides
Across the kitchen floor
Looking for food
Is stepped on, everything lost

A tramp holds his hand out
Looking for money
For food, he says
Wary passers-by know better

The single mother
Works all hours
To earn money to buy the food
For three starving infants

The lion's distended belly
Of three days ago
Gorging on a gnu
Now empty and hungry again

The Wall Street financier
His belly always rotund
Satisfies his hunger
With a hedge and fries

A restaurant in Beijing
Serves course after course
To the drunken elite
And throws away the rest

Rubble in Aleppo
Mud slides in Mexico
Floods in Bangladesh
No food or water for millions

Hunger for some
Distaste for others
Feast or famine
Or famine on famine

North Carolina, USA
May 2014

MANIFESTO

There are elections in many parts of the world; we see on a regular basis just how problematic these can be.

Zuma re-elected
Nothing will change
Modi elected
Cataclysms open up
But for Thailand, Ukraine
Egypt and Syria
And half of the world
Pretensions of democracy
As good as it gets

North Carolina, USA
May 2014

KILLING THE SPECIAL RELATIONSHIP

The British government makes an educational policy decision: remove most American literature from schools' reading lists!

———————

To kill the mocking bird
From the British curriculum
To say that mice and men
Are not good enough for Oxford
Is to denude
Shakespeare from Harvard
And Milton from Princeton
The Atlantic is a bridge
Not a wall of literary fire

North Carolina, USA
May 2014

THOSE WHO THINK FOR THEMSELVES

Still with education, there is a tendency, when you get a little older, to believe that standards are slipping and that outcomes, that is the intelligence and abilities of educated people, are not the same as they were. This temptation is very strong sometimes.

———————

The language of today
Strange vehicles of fame
Ten thousand re-tweets
Eighty blogs, no comments
Viral is good
Followers and friends of nothing
Add up
A few YouTube minutes
Shoot you to stardom
There is fluff in the clouds

The résumé is measured
Not in achievement
But in manipulation
Of others' thoughts
Careers often lost not gained
Through short missives
Sent without control

Real neural networks
Lead to brain power
Impaired internetworks
Take away that power
To think for oneself
Substituting garbage for wisdom

North Carolina, USA
May 2014

D-DAY

The 70th anniversary of D-Day needs no introduction. The pattern of war has changed, and this type of action is unlikely to be seen again, but these momentous events in history should never be forgotten.

For seventy years he stood proud
Never forgetting
Never really remembering
His momentous defining day

Young, just seventeen
Had to become a man
That decisive day

Delivered to a beach in Normandy
Heavily protected
That difficult day

Men all around blown apart or asunder
He struggled ashore
On that destructive day

They fought and fought
Sandhills and minefields
Never stopping, never giving up
That diabolical day

Now he stands
A cemetery of remembrance
Grateful his Queen came to see

She remembered that day
Today's politicians not even born
They struggle to relate to
The immensity of death that day

But they came
And duly extolled
Their thanks and
Their feelings on destiny day

Hope that the presence
Of our man
Impresses these leaders
Never, never, repeat
That damned D-day

North Carolina, USA
June 2014

LIFE AND SOUL OF THE PARTY

*We live under one of the helicopter flight paths to a major hospital
that has a transplant centre.*

A heart passing through the sky
Blades overhead
Unsuspecting parties below

Beneficial carnage
Begins with a wreck
A straight line starts with death
Hopefully life at the other end

Permission tenderly sought
Distraughtly given
Kidneys to Winston
Liver to Charlotte
Heart to Philly
Brain going nowhere just yet
Except for the grave

But where is the soul?
Does it go to the grave as well,
Or to the life-support hospitals?

Can a soul be divided this way?
No-one knows
It surely wasn't consulted
Body partitioned
Soul forgotten

Winston-Salem, North Carolina, USA
June 2014

THE SANCTITY OF EVIL

The daily news of terrorist-delivered death and destruction
is heartbreaking; the events defy all logic to the majority of us.

We are told of a love
That passeth all understanding
We want to believe
That this is so

The inexplicable patterns of nature
Can only unfold this way
From conception
To movement in the firmament
The heavenly control
Of water, fire, earth and air
To the benefit of all

No need for a big bang
Or a Higgs Nobel boson
The courses and causes of life
Have been achieved
Through motivation and love
That passeth all understanding

But there is something else
That passeth all understanding
Or so I believe

We know we are not all the same
Life would be dull if we were
Biologically impossible
Unless all created simultaneously
Not just in its likeness
But by the genes of our maker

In the delicate arrangement of humanity
Built on strong trunks but unsteady branches
Strands are broken
In chromosomes, genes and beings
Houses of cards are challenged
Yielding ripples or even volcanoes
Within this harmonious world of love

Unintended by nature, I'm sure
Aberrations beget evil
Actions of this force
Are committed which
Passeth all understanding

At some point
Before Genesis
At the birth of Homo erectus
Evil genes mutated

I have seen a lion bring down a springbok
Not far away, off the coast
Sharks throw into the air seal pups
Before tearing them apart
A python winds around a warthog
Hyenas laugh at their steal
Are these acts of evil?
No, just nature's hunger

Deer, or elk or moose
Lock horns with each other
Old bull elephants
Defend against imposters
Often to the death
Are these acts of evil?
No, just procreation control

Where in the animal preserve
Is ever a hint
Of the evil of men?
True, some dogs hunt deer and foxes

Not for their food we note
Bears fight each other when baited
The evil of man
Can be passed on
Through training and denial

Today, Boko Haram
Gleefully degrade young women
Captured in the name of Islam
Leaders in Syria
Content with razing their cities
In the name of what?

Russian leaders in Ukraine
Proclaim Stalin as the saviour of the world
Bosnia, Rwanda, Biafra, Hitler, ISIS
We know that evil exists
Profoundly in mankind
Way beyond our understanding

North Carolina, USA
July 2014

PROMISES IN THE WIND

*On a brief visit to Hong Kong to advise government on research strategy,
the tension with the mainland is palpable; soon to lead to unrest
and student occupations.*

Uncertain people
Under threatening clouds
Anxiousness in Kowloon
As stormy weather
Drives down from the Pearl Delta
Between and within the hills
And islands of Hong Kong
Dividing and conquering the nervous
Who had been promised stability
As the British civilly left

Now the epicentre of a clash
Between tectonic plates
Of capitalism and communism
Could the Chinese hold
The promise of democracy
Amid the turbulence of Beijing power?

Islands and seas from
Japan, Taiwan and Vietnam
Occupied in support of capital
Are feeling the wrath
Of the dragon, the new behemoth
Will the clouds disperse
Allowing the territories to stand firm
Or will they too surrender?

Hong Kong
August 2014

TODAY'S TOMORROW

*Spring comes very belatedly to North Carolina, but omens
on the world stage are not good.*

———————

Why is that daffodil smiling
At the end of a cold winter
The cardinal in its Sunday best red
Swooping in search of its mate
Why are irises pushing upwards
Prunus ready to burst
Green buds pregnant on trees
Ferns disgorging their winter's brown clothes
Squirrels digging for nuts
As if there is no tomorrow

For it seems to us there is no tomorrow
Of the shape of yesterday
A suicidal plane in France
Yemen disintegrates
Putin recapturing the east of Europe
The White House and Bibi's house
Collide with nuclear intent
Zuma destroys Mandela's legacy
Racism alive and kicking in the US Midwest
ISIS more dominant than the UN
Migrants and refugees drowning everywhere
Ebola conquered by MSF not WHO
Cruz starts his two-year wasteful campaign

Tomorrow should not be like this
Sure, each century has its moments
The Black Death, European revolutions
Darfur and Rwanda, the World Wars
But there were bright sides too
And more often
Where is the brightness of today's tomorrow?

North Carolina, USA
April 2015